THE F

To DAVID

THE FED FLUNKS

My Speech at the
New York Federal Reserve Bank

Robert Wenzel

Gallatin House

Gallatin House

FIRST EDITION May 2014

ISBN 978-1-312-04723-5

Library of Congress Cataloging-in-Publication Data

Wenzel, Robert

The Fed Flunks: my speech at the New York Federal Reserve bank/Robert Wenzel

Subject headings:

Banks and banking-United States.

Federal Reserve banks-History.

Monetary policy.

Money-History.

United States-Economic policy.

Cover design by Thomas Rossini

Published by Gallatin House LLC

ACKNOWLEDGEMENTS

Special thanks to the following, who helped me research and collect data for the my Fed speech: Stephen Davis, Bob English, Jon Lyons, Ash Navabi, Joseph Nelson, Nick Nero and Antony Zegers. And thanks to Joseph Sauer and Chris Rossini , who reviewed and commented on parts of the material herein.

CONTENTS

ROBERT WENZEL

INTRODUCTION

Since I am an outspoken critic of the Federal Reserve, many people have asked how I ended up delivering a speech at the Federal Reserve Bank of New York, arguably the key regional bank of the Fed. The New York Fed houses all the trading operations of the Federal Reserve. This means that all the buying and selling of securities and other assets that the Fed does, it does through the New York branch. And some of the Fed's top economists do their research from this branch. The president of the New York Fed is considered by many to be the most powerful of all regional Fed bank presidents. Timothy Geithner, before he became the United States Secretary of the Treasury, served as the president of the New York Fed.

So how did I get invited to deliver my anti-Fed views there?

It all started when New York Federal Reserve economist Simon Potter, Executive Vice President and Director of Economic Research at the New York Federal Reserve, wrote that the Fed had missed the boat in recognizing the housing bubble and the 2008 financial crisis as it was developing.

He mentioned a couple of economists that had warned about the bubble, but did not mention me. I emailed him and pointed out that in 2004 I had written[1] a critique of a paper by New York Federal Reserve economists Richard Peach and Jonathan McCarthy who argued that there was no housing bubble[2]. I further noted in the email that in real time at my web site, EconomicPolicyJournal.com, I had warned during the summer of 2008 of a developing financial crisis. This warning proved quite prescient as the economy and financial markets started to come apart at the seams in September of 2008.

Potter forwarded my email to Peach and a series of back and forth emails over some months ensued. Here is some of that correspondence:

November 11, 2011

Dear Mr. Wenzel,

Simon Potter forwarded to me your comment on his recent post on the Liberty Street Economics blog. As you refer to my paper with Jonathan McCarthy quite extensively in your comment, I wanted to take a moment to respond.

If I understand your comments correctly, you indicated that you warned that there was a housing bubble in 2004 and 2005 under a pen name, and then again in 2008. This suggests that you thought the 2004 level of prices were in bubble territory, whereas we though they were supported by fundamentals. We did not conclude in our paper that home prices could rise another 35% to 40%, which they did, and still be supported by fundamentals.

I would like to refer you to the following chart which plots the average FHFA home price by state for 2004 versus the level of 2011Q2. You will note that in most states, as well as for the nation as a whole, recent levels of home prices remain equal to or slightly above the 2004 average level. There are some notable exceptions, in particular Florida, Nevada, California, and Arizona.

Of course, prices may fall further. But as it stands at the moment, your call in 2004 that the level of home prices was in bubble territory does not appear to have been correct.

Regards

Dick Peach

Richard W. Peach

Senior Vice President

THE FED FLUNKS

Federal Reserve Bank of New York

33 Liberty Street

New York, NY 10045

February 28, 2012

Dear Dr. Peach,

I have other questions with regard to your ingenious argument that calls Florida, Nevada, California, and Arizona "exceptions". California? Florida?

However, you yourself seem to draw the line at the 2004 national price level. The Standard & Poor's/Case-Shiller home-price index out this morning shows that prices are now, at best, at 2002 levels.

I quote AP on the Schiller report:

"Prices have fallen 34 percent nationwide since the housing bust, back to 2002 levels."

Are you at this point willing to concede that I was correct about my [view]?

Regards,

Bob Wenzel

February 28, 2012

Please do come in for lunch. Perhaps you would like to give a seminar as well. Do you have plans to be in New York any time soon?

Richard W. Peach

Senior Vice President

Federal Reserve Bank of New York

33 Liberty Street

New York, NY 10045

March 2, 2102

Dear Dr Peach,

Thanks again for inviting me to the New York Fed. I am working on penciling in my schedule for March and April. Do you have a specific date in mind, so that I can block it off on my calendar?

Best regards,

Bob Wenzel

March 2, 2102

How about sometime over the three days of April 25, 26, or 27. Also, would you like to give a presentation or just have a more informal discussion over lunch?

Have a good weekend.

Richard W. Peach

Senior Vice President

ROBERT WENZEL

Federal Reserve Bank of New York

33 Liberty Street

New York, NY 10045

March 3, 2012

Dear Dr. Peach,

April 25 would work best for me. It would probably be best if I deliver a short formal presentation since there are specific points I would like to make in a more orderly fashion. This could be followed immediately by lunch, where a more informal discussion could be carried on.

Best regards,

Bob

THE FED FLUNKS

April 17, 2012

Bob,

I have made a reservation for us for lunch at 12:30 pm in our Liberty Room. Please arrive at our 33 Liberty Street entrance at around that time and I will meet you. I have invited several of my colleagues, including Simon Potter and Jonathan McCarthy, to join us. I look forward to meeting you.

Regards

Dick

Richard W. Peach

Senior Vice President

Federal Reserve Bank of New York

33 Liberty Street

New York, NY 10045

The next thing I received was a copy of a formal email invitation that also went out to a number of other economists at the New York Fed.

Not surprisingly, someone at the Fed, who received the invitation, tried to sabotage the event. In short order, the formal invitation was cancelled, but Peach, ever the gentlemen, told me that he would see to it that the invitation would stand and I would have the opportunity to deliver my speech.

I was really unsure if the event would actually take place. Indeed, even on the day of the event, after passing through two security checkpoints at the Fed, I wasn't sure if it would take place, but at that point, since I was in the building, lunch or no lunch, I was going to deliver the speech, even if I had to deliver it in the Fed's men's room.

Fortunately, that didn't have to happen. A security guard called Peach and he came down to greet me and escorted me to the Liberty Room (I know, "Liberty" Room at the Fed? Don't get me started). On the way, he said that the other economists were "delayed at a meeting, but would join us later." (This did not surprise me.)

In the Liberty Room, he had reserved two tables, each set for 12 people. Thus, he was expecting attendance of up to 24. He proposed that we start eating before the rest of the economists arrived, so that I could be done eating and deliver the speech while the others ate. In time, the Vice President of Macroeconomic and Monetary Studies Function, Jonathan McCarthy, arrived. Peach was the Senior Vice President of Macroeconomic and Monetary Studies Function, these were two of the three key economists from the NY Fed that I wanted to hear my speech. The other would have been Potter, but it did not appear he was coming.

At this point, I just wanted to get my message out. I knew the internet would take care of the rest. I had pre-scheduled the speech to get posted at EconomiPolicyJournal.com, just as I was delivering it. (Just like the Fed publishes Fed chair speeches at the Fed site as they are delivered). So I said to Peach and McCarthy, "Look I have prepared formal remarks and I want to get them out in this building." As I started reading my speech, I could see tension on the faces of Peach and McCarthy, especially McCarthy. He was getting upset and then visibly furious at what I was saying. Peach did not display any obvious reaction beyond the tension.

As soon as I finished my speech, and to defuse the tension, I asked an immediate question of McCarthy and Peach. I had used Austrian Business Cycle Theory as the foundation for my speech and so I asked them if they thought ABCT had a legitimate case to make.

The slow response came from Peach who said that there had been worse crashes in the economy before the start

10

of the Fed. (Side note, the great Austrian school economist, Murray Rothbard in his book, *A History of Money and Banking in the United States: The Colonial Era to World War II*[3] showed the link between pre-Federal Reserve government central banks and the boom bust cycle.) I then asked Peach (a 20 year plus veteran of the Fed) if he was familiar with Austrian economics. He said that in college he had taken two history of economics courses and then said that the Austrian school is part of the classical tradition. This told me that he was not aware of the important distinctions between the Austrian school and classical economics (and also the neo-classical tradition).

Later on during our discussion, Peach remarked that he understood the Austrian school and that they were the group that wanted a constant increase in the money supply and developed the equation PV=MT. This, of course, is not the Austrian view, but a view held by the Chicago school. Thus, in one swoop, Peach demonstrated not only his lack of knowledge of Austrian views on monetary policy, but also confusion about Austrian school versus Chicago school theory.

To diffuse the tension a bit more, when McCarthy made a particularly Keynesian school statement, I said, "It does not sound like you are going to be walking out of here with me after lunch like I recommended in the speech." That brought laughter.

At another point, I told the story of how in a phone
conversation with Lew Rockwell, founder and chairman
of the Mises Institute[4], Lew and I were discussing why I
had received an invitation by the Fed and Lew said,
"They are probably sick and tired of all those boring
speeches that they have to listen to." That really brought
laughter.

A good deal of the Q&A was about my Rothbardian
view that prices should be allowed to decline. They were
really fascinated by this view and clearly had never
heard it before. McCarthy raised the question of how
falling prices would impact assets. The answer is, of
course, that an asset is valued based on its discounted
value stream and that falling prices would be taken into
account in the discounted present value models.

Overall, I was simply amazed at the lack of knowledge
about the Austrian school by these senior Fed
economists. It was very close to non-existent. This
points out the extremely important work being done by
the Mises Institute. The number of students with an
understanding of Austrian school economics is
increasing at an exponential rate. I can't imagine that
future economists, even those who work for the Fed,
won't have some acquaintance with Austrian economics
thanks to MI.

My experience at the Fed points out the importance of
intellectual debate and study. Clearly, the economists
that I met at the Fed were brought up in an intellectual

tunnel, where they had no exposure to Austrian economic theory. They read and study within a limited range of writers. In other words, they are a perfect example of what the Austrian school economist, and Nobel laureate, F. A. Hayek called 'the lost generation of economists[5]." But they were very curious about my view.

Peach asked me how I knew the housing market was going to crash. I responded that because of Austrian theory, I understood that money created by the Fed enters the economy at specific points and that it was obvious the housing market was one of the points. I told him that I also knew that this would eventually result in price inflation (as the money spread through the economy) and that, at that point, the Fed would slow printing and the housing market would collapse, which is just what occurred.

I suspect that at the top of the Fed, there are some very evil types who understand the game is to protect the banksters, but I don't think that is the view held by the outer-circle of Fed economists that include McCarthy and Peach. They have been brought up in the system and they don't ask questions that threaten their paychecks and they do their work strictly by developing models within the Keynesian framework.

If you set a firecracker under them, like I did with the speech I delivered and then treat them with respect while discussing their opposing views and lighten things up a bit after the firecracker has gone off, perhaps some impact will be made to the very limited universe of economic thinking that they have been exposed to their entire professional lives. Even more important, hopefully my speech will help budding economics students to understand that the Fed propaganda machine claims lots of justifications for their money printing machines which when looked at closely cannot be justified,. The greater the number that understand the failures of Fed thinking and operations, the closer we will be to ending the Fed.

As I expected, the speech had its biggest impact on the internet.

Many, many websites have asked permission to reprint my speech. I estimate that given the audience of the web sites that have reposted the speech and those that have come directly to EPJ to read the speech, approximately 1,000,000 people have read the speech. An author has requested permission to reprint it as a chapter in his upcoming book. Jeff Rowberg has created an audio version. I have been interviewed on radio shows about the speech. An investment advisory firm has requested permission to print it and send it to all its clients. And Tyler Durden at Zero Hedge[6] had these kind words to say about it:

> In perhaps the most courageous (and likely must-read for future economists) speech ever given inside the New York Fed's shallowed hallowed walls, Economic Policy Journal's

Robert Wenzel delivered the truth, the whole truth, and nothing but the truth to the monetary priesthood. Gracious from the start, Wenzel takes the Keynesian clap-trappers to task on almost every nonsensical and oblivious decision they have made in recent years.

"My views, I suspect, differ from beginning to end... I stand here confused as to how you see the world so differently than I do. I simply do not understand most of the thinking that goes on here at the Fed and I do not understand how this thinking can go on when in my view it smacks up against reality."

and further...

"I scratch my head that somehow your conclusions about unemployment are so different than mine and that you call for the printing of money to boost 'demand'. A call, I add, that since the founding of the Federal Reserve has resulted in an increase of the money supply by 12,230%."

But his closing was tremendous:

"Let's have one good meal here. Let's make it a feast. Then I ask you, I plead with you, I beg you all, walk out of here with me, never to come back. It's the moral and ethical thing to do. Nothing good goes on in this place. Let's lock the doors and leave the building to the spiders, moths and four-legged rats."

The great historian Ralph Raico emailed to say, "Bob, your talk to the Fed was absolutely brilliant!" Libertarian great Walter Block emailed and said:"That is not a 'good' Austrian critique of Keynesianism and the Fed, it is an EXCELLENT one" The important Misesian scholar Richard Ebeling emailed, "I read your speech at the Fed, and your postscript. Brilliant! Just the type of talk that should be given in a place like that, and superbly constructed and articulated !!!!"

Mainstream media has maintained radio silence.

In addition to publishing my Fed Speech, in this booklet, I have also included, as Chapter 2, the original critique I wrote of the Peach-McCarthy paper. Chapter 3 is my *real time* commentary, during the summer of 2008 at *EconomicPolicyJournal.com,* as money supply slowed--- just as I predicted in my Peach-McCarthy paper and just before the financial crisis came into full bloom in the Fall of 2008. In Chapter 4, I discuss how I track money supply in a way that has allowed me to get a good sense for trends in the economy and allowed me to warn about the housing bubble and the 2008 financial crisis.

Finally, I include an appendix, which is a technical point for economists on why I include money market funds in my calculation of money supply.

Robert Wenzel

San Francisco

March 5. 20014

THE FED FLUNKS

CHAPTER 1

My Speech Delivered at the New York Federal Reserve Bank

Delivered on April 25, 2012 at the invitation of the New York Federal Reserve Bank

Thank you very much for inviting me to speak here at the New York Federal Reserve Bank.

Intellectual discourse is, of course, extraordinarily valuable in reaching truth. In this sense, I welcome the opportunity to discuss my views on the economy and monetary policy and how they may differ with those of you here at the Fed.

That said, I suspect my views are so different from those of you here today that my comments will be a complete failure in convincing you to do what I believe should be done, which is to close down the entire Federal Reserve System

THE FED FLUNKS

My views, I suspect, differ from beginning to end. From the proper methodology[7] to be used in the science of economics, to the manner in which the macro-economy functions, to the role of the Federal Reserve, and to the accomplishments of the Federal Reserve, I stand here confused as to how you see the world so differently than I do.

I simply do not understand most of the thinking that goes on here at the Fed and I do not understand how this thinking can go on when in my view it smacks up against reality.

Please allow me to begin with methodology, I hold the view developed by such great economic thinkers as Ludwig von Mises, Friedrich Hayek and Murray Rothbard that there are no constants in the science of economics similar to those in the physical sciences.

In the science of physics, we know that water freezes at 32 degrees. We can predict with immense accuracy exactly how far a rocket ship will travel filled with 500 gallons of fuel. There is preciseness because there are constants, which do not change and upon which equations can be constructed.

There are no such constants in the field of economics since the science of economics deals with human action, which can change at any time. If potato prices remain the same for 10 weeks, it does not mean they will be the same the following day. I defy anyone in this room to provide me with a constant in the field of economics that has the same unchanging constancy that exists in the fields of physics or chemistry.

And yet, in paper after paper written here at the Federal Reserve, I see equations built as though constants do exist. It is as if one were to assume a constant relationship existed between interest rates here and in Russia and throughout the world, and create equations based on this belief and then attempt to trade based on these equations. That was tried and the result was the blow up of the fund, Long Term Capital Management[8], a blow up that resulted in high level meetings in this very building.

It is as if traders assumed a given default rate was constant for subprime mortgage paper and traded on that belief, only to see it blow up in their faces, as it did, again, with intense meetings being held in this very building[9].

Yet, the equations, assuming constants, continue to be published in papers throughout the Fed system.

I also find curious the general belief in the Keynesian model of the economy that somehow results in the belief that demand drives the economy, rather than production.

THE FED FLUNKS

I look out at the world and see iPhones, iPads, microwave ovens, flat screen televisions, which suggest to me that it is production that boosts an economy. Without production of these goods and millions of other items, where would we be? Yet, the Keynesians in this room will reply, "But you need demand to buy these products." And I will reply, "Do you not believe in supply and demand? Do you not believe that products once made will adjust to a market clearing price?"

Further, I will argue that the price of the factors of production will adjust to prices at the consumer level and that thus the markets at all levels will clear. Again do you believe in supply and demand or not?

I know that most of you on some academic level believe in the theory of supply and demand and how market setting prices result, but yet you deny them in your macro thinking about the economy.

You will say to me that prices are sticky on the downside, especially labor prices and therefore that a central bank must pump money to get the economy going. And, I will look on in amazement as your fellow Keynesian brethren in the government create an environment of sticky non-downward bending wages.

The economist Robert Murphy reports that President Herbert Hoover continually pressured businessmen to not lower wages.[10]

He quoted Hoover in a speech delivered to a group of businessmen:

> In this country there has been a concerted and determined effort on the part of government and business... to prevent any reduction in wages.

He then reports that FDR actually outdid Hoover by seeking to "raise wages rates rather than merely put a floor under them."

I ask you, with presidents actively conducting policies that attempt to defy supply and demand and prop up wages, are you really surprised that wages were sticky downward during the Great Depression?

In present day America, the government focus has changed a bit. In the new focus, the government attempts much more to prop up the unemployed by extended payments for not working. Is it really a surprise that unemployment is so high when you pay people not to work? The 2010 Nobel Prize was awarded to economists for their studies which showed that, and I quote from the Nobel press release[11] announcing the award:

One conclusion is that more generous unemployment benefits give rise to higher unemployment and longer search times.

Don't you think it would make more sense to stop these policies which are a direct factor in causing unemployment, than to add to the mess and devalue the currency by printing more money to attempt to remedy the unemployment situation?

I scratch my head that somehow your conclusions about unemployment are so different than mine and that you call for the printing of money to boost "demand". A call, I add, that since the founding of the Federal Reserve has resulted in an increase of the money supply by 12,230%.

I also must scratch my head at the view that the Federal Reserve should maintain a stable price level. What is wrong with having falling prices across the economy, like we now have in the computer sector, the flat screen television sector and the cell phone sector? Why, I ask, do you want stable prices? And, oh by the way, how's that stable price thing going for you here at the Fed?

Since the start of the Fed, prices have increased at the consumer level by 2,241% [12]. That's not me misspeaking, I will repeat, since the start of the Fed, prices have increased at the consumer level by 2,241%.

So you then might tell me that stable prices are only a secondary goal of the Federal Reserve and that your real goal is to prevent serious declines in the economy but, since the start of the Fed, there have been 18 recessions including the Great Depression and the most recent Great Recession. These downturns have resulted in stock market crashes, tens of millions of unemployed and untold business bankruptcies.

I wonder how you think the Fed is any type of success when all this has occurred.

I am especially confused, since Austrian Business Cycle Theory (ABCT), developed by Ludwig von Mises, F.A. Hayek and Murray Rothbard, warned about all these things. According to ABCT, it is central bank money printing that causes the business cycle and, again you here at the Fed have certainly done that by increasing the money supply. Can you imagine the distortions in the economy caused by the Fed by this massive money printing?

According to ABCT, if you print money, those sectors where the money goes will boom, stop printing and those sectors will crash. Fed printing tends to find its way to Wall Street and other capital goods sectors first, thus it is no surprise to Austrian school economists that the crashes are most dramatic in these sectors, such as the stock market and real estate sectors. The economist Murray Rothbard in his book *America's Great Depression* [13] went into painstaking detail outlining how the changes in money supply growth resulted in the Great Depression.

On a more personal level, as the recent crisis was developing here, I warned throughout the summer of 2008 of the impending crisis. On July 11, 2008 at EconomicPolicyJournal.com, I wrote[14]:

> SUPER ALERT: Dramatic Slowdown In Money Supply Growth

> After growing at near double digit rates for months, money growth has slowed dramatically. Annualized money growth over the last 3 months is only 5.2%. Over the last two months, there has been zero growth in the M2NSA money measure.

> This is something that must be watched carefully. If such a dramatic slowdown continues, a severe recession is inevitable.

> We have never seen such a dramatic change in money supply growth from a double digit climb to 5% growth. Does Bernanke have any clue as to what the hell he is doing?

On July 20, 2008, I wrote[15]:

> I have previously noted that over the last two months money supply has been collapsing. M2NSA has gone from double digit growth to nearly zero growth.

> A review of the credit situation appears worse. According to recent Fed data, for the 13 weeks ended June 25, bank credit (securities and loans) contracted at an annual rate of 7.9%.

> There has been a minor blip up since June 25 in both credit growth and M2NSA, but the growth rates remain extremely slow.

> If a dramatic turnaround in these numbers doesn't happen within the next few weeks, we are going to have to warn of a possible Great Depression style downturn.

Yet, just weeks before these warnings from me, Chairman Bernanke, while the money supply growth was crashing, had a decidedly much more optimistic outlook. In a speech on June 9, 2008, At the Federal Reserve Bank of Boston's 53rd Annual Economic Conference[16], he said:

I would like to provide a brief update on the outlook for the economy and policy, beginning with the prospects for growth. Despite the unwelcome rise in the unemployment rate that was reported last week, the recent incoming data, taken as a whole, have affected the outlook for economic activity and employment only modestly. Indeed, although activity during the current quarter is likely to be weak, the risk that the economy has entered a substantial downturn appears to have diminished over the past month or so. Over the remainder of 2008, the effects of monetary and fiscal stimulus, a gradual ebbing of the drag from residential construction, further progress in the repair of financial and credit markets, and still-solid demand from abroad should provide some offset to the headwinds that still face the economy.

I believe the Great Recession that followed is still fresh enough in our minds so it is not necessary to recount in detail as to whose forecast, mine or the chairman's, was more accurate.

I am also confused by many other policy making steps here at the Federal Reserve. There have been more changes in monetary policy direction during the Bernanke era then at any other time in the modern era of the Fed. Not under Arthur Burns, not under G. William Miller, not under Paul Volcker, not under Alan Greenspan have there been so many dramatically

shifting Fed monetary policy moves. Under Chairman
Bernanke there have been significant changes in
direction of the money supply growth FIVE different
times. Thus, for me, I am not at all surprised at the
current stop and go economy. The current erratic
monetary policy makes it exceedingly difficult for
businessmen to make any long term plans. Indeed, in my
own Daily Alert on the economy[17] I find it extremely
difficult to give long term advice, when in short periods
I have seen three month annualized M2 money growth
go from near 20% to near zero, and then in another
period see it go from 25% to 6% . [18]

I am also confused by many of the monetary programs
instituted by Chairman Bernanke. For example,
Operation Twist.

This is not the first time an Operation Twist was tried. an
Operation Twist was tried in 1961, at the start of the
Kennedy Administration[19] A paper[20] was written by
three Federal Reserve economists in 2004 that, in part,
examined the 1960's Operation Twist

Their conclusion:

> A second well-known historical episode
> involving the attempted manipulation of the
> term structure was so-called Operation Twist.
> Launched in early 1961 by the incoming
> Kennedy Administration, Operation Twist was

intended to raise short-term rates (thereby promoting capital inflows and supporting the dollar) while lowering, or at least not raising, long-term rates. (Modigliani and Sutch 1966).... The two main actions of Operation Twist were the use of Federal Reserve open market operations and Treasury debt management operations..Operation Twist is widely viewed today as having been a failure, largely due to classic work by Modigliani and Sutch....

However, Modigliani and Sutch also noted that Operation Twist was a relatively small operation, and, indeed, that over a slightly longer period the maturity of outstanding government debt rose significantly, rather than falling...Thus, Operation Twist does not seem to provide strong evidence in either direction as to the possible effects of changes in the composition of the central bank's balance sheet....

We believe that our findings go some way to refuting the strong hypothesis that nonstandard policy actions, including quantitative easing and targeted asset purchases, cannot be successful in a modern industrial economy. However, the effects of such policies remain quantitatively quite uncertain.

ROBERT WENZEL

One of the authors of this 2004 paper was Federal Reserve Chairman Bernanke. Thus, I have to ask, "What the hell is Chairman Bernanke doing implementing such a program, since it is his paper that states the program was a failure according to Modigliani, and his paper implies that a larger test would be required to determine true performance?"

I ask, is the Chairman using the United States economy as a lab with Americans as the lab rats to test his intellectual curiosity about such things as Operation Twist?

Further, I am very confused by the response of Chairman Bernanke to questioning by Congressman Ron Paul. To a seemingly near off the cuff question by Congressman Paul on Federal Reserve money provided to the Watergate burglars, Chairman Bernanke contacted the Inspector General's Office of the Federal Reserve and requested an investigation[21]. Yet, the congressman has regularly asked about the gold certificates held by the Federal Reserve[22] and whether the gold at Fort Knox backing up the certificates will be audited. Yet there have been no requests by the Chairman to the Treasury for an audit of the gold. This I find very odd. The Chairman calls for a major investigation of what can only be a historical point of interest but fails to seek out any confirmation on a point that would be of vital interest to many present day Americans.

In this very building, deep in the underground vaults, sits billions of dollars of gold, held by the Federal Reserve for foreign governments. The Federal Reserve gives regular tours of these vaults, even to school children.[23] Yet, America's gold is off limits to seemingly everyone and has never been properly audited. Doesn't that seem odd to you? If nothing else, does anyone at the Fed know the quality and fineness of the gold at Fort Knox?

In conclusion, it is my belief that from start to finish the Fed is a failure. I believe faulty methodology is used, I believe that the justification for the Fed, to bring price and economic stability, has never been a success. I repeat, prices since the start of the Fed have climbed by 2,241% and there have been over the same period 18 recessions. No one seems to care at the Fed about the gold supposedly backing up the gold certificates on the Fed balance sheet. The emperor has no clothes. Austrian Business cycle theorists are regularly ignored by the Fed, yet they have the best records with regard to spotting overall downturns, and further they specifically recognized the developing housing bubble. Let it not be forgotten that in 2004, two economists here at the New York Fed wrote a paper[24] denying there was a housing bubble. I responded to the paper[25] and wrote:

> The faulty analysis by [these] Federal Reserve economists... may go down in financial history as the greatest forecasting error since Irving Fisher declared in 1929, just prior to the stock market crash, that stocks prices looked to be at a permanently high plateau.

Data, released recently, show housing prices have
crashed to 2002 levels.[26]

I will now give you more warnings about the economy.

The noose is tightening on your organization, vast
amounts of money printing are now required to keep
your manipulated economy afloat. It will ultimately
result in huge price inflation, or, if you stop printing,
another massive economic crash will occur. There is no
other way out.

Again, thank you for inviting me. You have prepared
food, so I will not be rude, I will stay and eat.

Let's have one good meal here. Let's make it a feast.
Then I ask you, I plead with you, I beg you all, walk out
of here with me, never to come back. It's the moral and
ethical thing to do. Nothing good goes on in this place.
Let's lock the doors and leave the building to the
spiders, moths and four-legged rats.

THE FED FLUNKS

CHAPTER 2

WHAT CAUSED THE HOUSING BUBBLE

The following is the critique I wrote in 2004, when the Fed economists, Johnathan McCarthy and Richard W.Peach, wrote a paper arguing that there was no housing bubble. History, of course, proved me correct. A review of my commentary in this paper shows why I saw the housing crsis developing and also why the Fed economists missed it.

Federal Reserve Bank of New York economists, Jonathan McCarthy and Richard W. Peach, have just completed a new study with the title, Are Home Prices The Next 'Bubble'? [27]In the study they clearly reach the conclusion that no such bubble exists.

We believe that their conclusion has been reached because of faulty analysis.

In their study, they reach their conclusion by eliminating from consideration, at the start, the primary cause of the real estate bubble out of existence before they even begin their analysis, and by ignoring the structural components of the current housing finance market that will make any price decline even worse than it would otherwise be.

THE FED FLUNKS

They tell us that they are using the Joseph Stiglitz definition of a bubble:

> "If the reason the price is high today is only because investors believe that the selling price will be higher tomorrow-when 'fundamental' factors do not seem to justify such a price -then a bubble exists."

They then proceed to conduct an analysis of the current real estate market and tell us that a key factor pushing real estate prices higher is that nominal interest rates have been dropping. They reach the conclusion that because of this "fundamental factor" of low nominal interest rates, higher housing prices are justified.

But does this mean real estate prices will not drop? Our answer is emphatically, "No." Indeed, McCarthy-Peach report that "since 1995, real home prices have increased about 36 percent, roughly double the increase of previous home price booms in the late 1970s and late 1980s." We view this increase as largely the result of the Federal Reserve's lowering of interest rates and the pumping of liquidity into the banking system, thus producing the byproduct of higher housing prices. But by incorporating falling nominal interest rates as a "fundamental factor" that cannot be a cause of a bubble, McCarthy-Peach have literally removed the driving cause of the current bubble from being taken into consideration.

The multi-year liquidity burst from the Federal Reserve that has pushed interest rates lower sets the stage for major price inflation down the road. It is this price inflation which then makes it difficult for the Federal Reserve to continue to keep up the liquidity creation that is fueling the real estate boom, and forces the Fed to begin to fight price inflation by raising interest rates, which will ultimately lead to the bursting of the housing bubble.

We also disagree with McCarthy and Peach when they argue that the Federal Reserve is only likely to raise interest rates during a period of strong economic growth.

This, in our view, is a Keynesian canard that should have been buried during the late 1970s to early 1980s, a period of rising inflation, rising interest rates and an economy in recession. It is, in fact, this 1970s-1980's scenario of rising interest rates, rising inflation and an economy in recession that is the most likely scenario we see as occurring in the near future as opposed to the McCarthy-Peach scenario where they believe

"... that higher interest rates would not necessarily lead to a large decline in equilibrium home prices. [Because] In the current environment, rising rates probably would result from stronger employment and income growth. Therefore, while the contribution from user costs would

be negative, the economic-strength contribution would counteract it."

In truth, the only factor that will seemingly get the Fed's attention, and cause them to raise interest rates, is not whether there is "growth" in the economy, but to the degree price inflation begins to become obvious at the consumer level.

We are at the very early stages of the recognition by the Federal Reserve of such an inflationary environment. Thus the stage is set for the Fed to slowdown new liquidity entering the economy and to start raising interest rates.

This choking off of the monetary spigot will indeed impact the real estate sector, as this sector has been the strongest beneficiary of the Fed-induced multi-year growth in money supply.

Further, the current structure of many mortgage loans where no money down is acceptable and adjustable rate mortgages are popular, sets up the possibility that many may walk away from their current mortgage commitments down the road as interest rates begin to climb. Indeed, as ARM's rates become more and more burdensome and as housing prices begin to decline, walk away situations are likely to become quite prevalent, thus adding even more downward pressure to the housing market.

It is our conclusion, then, that by defining nominal interest rates as a fundamental factor and not as the Fed induced causal factor of the real estate boom, and by completely ignoring the structural features of current mortgage loans, McCarthy and Peach have blinded themselves to the real estate bubble that does exist. They have set themselves up for perhaps making the worst economic prediction since Irving Fisher declared in 1929, just prior to the stock market crash, that "stocks prices have reached what looks to be a permanently high plateau." [28]

So just when will housing prices begin to decline? A quarter point increase in the Fed Funds rate won't do it. In fact, keeping an eye on the Fed funds rate for a clue, as to when the real estate bubble will burst, is keeping an eye on the wrong end of the animal, so to speak. What needs to be monitored is how much of a slowdown in money growth, if any, is caused by the Feds gradual increase in interest rates. In the last 6 months M2 has grown at a rate of 7.1%. In the last year M2 has grown at a rate of 4.9%.

It is this growth in money supply that has been fueling the real estate boom. It is when this growth in money supply begins to slow in earnest to under 5%, as the Fed slowly begins to raise rates, that you will see the real estate bubble begin to burst and then cascade downward.

THE FED FLUNKS

At this point, it is not exactly clear how high the Fed will have to raise the Fed Funds rate to bring money growth to under 5%, but rest assured they will. The tremendous amount of new money the Fed has created over the last decade (a total increase in money supply of over 75%) is beginning to be reflected at the consumer level. This is when the Fed gets concerned about price inflation. But, this consumer level inflation isn't going to stop any time soon. You don't simply fight an inflation that was created by over a decade of money growth with one interest rate hike or two. The Fed is very late to the inflation fighting scene, so the Fed will be continuing to raise rates for a long time.

Indeed, they are so late on the scene because the Fed is responsible for the current housing boom and despite studies such as the McCarthy-Peach analysis, the Fed knows that it has entrapped many in the housing bubble and that, when the inflation fight gets serious, housing prices will begin to fall, causing great hardship for many.

CHAPTER 3

An Administration Keynesian Speaks of Failure, Failure and Failure (And an Alternative Examined)

The Washington Post's Dana Bank on September 1, 2010 reported[29] on the remarkable departing words of the chairman of President Obama's Council of Economic Advisers, Christina Romer. It is valuable to read her remarks side by side with my real time commentary leading up to the financial crisis. Bank wrote:

> Lunch at the National Press Club on Wednesday caused some serious indigestion.

> It wasn't the food; it was the entertainment. Christina Romer, chairman of President Obama's Council of Economic Advisers, was giving what was billed as her "valedictory" before she returns to teach at Berkeley, and she used the swan song to establish four points, each more unnerving than the last:

> She had no idea how bad the economic collapse would be. She still doesn't understand exactly why it was so bad. The response to the collapse was inadequate. And she doesn't have much of an idea about how to fix things.

What she did have was a binder full of scary
descriptions and warnings, offered with a perma-
smile and singsong delivery: "Terrible recession.
. . . Incredibly searing. . . . Dramatically below
trend. . . . Suffering terribly. . . . Risk of making
high unemployment permanent. . . . Economic
nightmare."

Anybody want dessert?

At week's end, Romer will leave the council
chairmanship after what surely has been the
most dismal tenure anybody in that post has had:
a loss of nearly 4 million jobs in a year and a
half. That's not Romer's fault; the financial
collapse occurred before she, and Obama, took
office. But she was the president's top economist
during a time when the administration
consistently underestimated the depth of the
economy's troubles - miscalculations that have
caused Americans to lose faith in the president
and the Democrats.

Romer had predicted that Obama's stimulus
package would keep the unemployment rate at 8
percent or less; it is now 9.5 percent. One of her
bosses, Vice President Biden, told Democrats in
January that "you're going to see, come the

spring, net increase in jobs every month." The
economy lost 350,000 jobs in June and July...

Romer's farewell luncheon had been scheduled
for the club's ballroom, but attendance was light
and the event was moved to a smaller room.
Romer, wearing a green suit, read brightly from
her text - a delivery at odds with the dark
material she was presenting. When she and her
colleagues began work, she acknowledged, they
did not realize "how quickly and strongly the
financial crisis would affect the economy." They
"failed to anticipate just how violent the
recession would be."

Even now, Romer said, mystery persists. "To
this day, economists don't fully understand why
firms cut production as much as they did or why
they cut labor so much more than they normally
would." Her defense was that "almost all
analysts were surprised by the violent reaction."

.

But were all analysts, in fact, surprised by the violent
reaction?

If ever there was a real world clue of the failure of
Keynesian economics, it is this departing speech by
Romer. She admits that Administration economists (all

Keynesians) missed forecasting the economic crisis and its severity, failed to immediately implement policies that would halt the downturn. And, further, at the time the Administration economists had no clue what would happen next.

It should be made clear that this was not a failure of economics, but of Keynesians economics

Ac the crisis developed, while viewing the economy through an Austrian school of economics perspective, I wrote in **early July 2008**[30]:

> After growing at near double digit rates for months, money growth has slowed dramatically. Annualized money growth over the last 3 months is only 5.2%. Over the last two months, there has been zero growth in the M2NSA money measure.

> This is something that must be watched carefully. If such a dramatic slowdown continues, a severe recession is inevitable.

> We have never seen such a dramatic change in money supply growth from a double digit climb to 5% growth. Does Bernanke have any clue as to what the hell he is doing?

Later in **July 2008**, I wrote[31]:

> I have previously noted that over the last two months money supply has been collapsing. M2NSA has gone from double digit growth to nearly zero growth.

> A review of the credit situation appears worse. According to recent Fed data, for the 13 weeks ended June 25, bank credit (securities and loans) contracted at an annual rate of 7.9%.

> There has been a minor blip up since June 25 in both credit growth and M2NSA, but the growth rates remain extremely slow.

> If a dramatic turnaround in these numbers doesn't happen within the next few weeks, we are going to have to warn of a possible Great Depression style downturn.

In **August 2008**, I wrote[32]:

> After growing at near double digit rates, Fed money supply growth over recent months has

slowed dramatically. Three month annualized M2NSA money growth is at 2.8%. If money growth remains this low we will be in a recession in no time.

On **September 4, 2008,** I wrote[33]:

ALERT: MUST READ Money Growth Plunges To 1.8%

The M2 money supply growth rate continues to plunge.

Data released today by the Fed show the annualized growth rate for the thirteen weeks ending August 25, 2008 for M2 is now at 1.8%. As we have emphasized, this is after early 2008 M2 money supply growth at double digit rates.

If the Fed doesn't reverse engines real fast, the economy will plunge into Depression-like conditions within months, if not weeks.

Extreme caution should be exercised with regard to all long term business decisions. Within six months the economy could look much different. Preserve cash.

Bottom line: I have no crystal ball that allows me to make these forecasts. It is simply consistent application of Austrian Business Cycle Theory, which views the economy in terms of interest rate manipulations and money flows that originate from central banks. This is in direct contrast to Keynesian aggregate demand analysis which takes into consideration the influence central banks have on *specific* sectors of the economy, and completely fails to understand that government deficit spending is simply a transfer of income from producers to non-producers.

Romer's remarkable farewell speech touches bases on all these problems with Keynesian economics

The real key to advancing the economy is for more and more people to understand that Romer's speech is, indeed, about Keynesian failure, that governments throughout the world operate on the failed Keynesian theories (No wonder it's a global crisis), but that there is an alternative method to view the economy, which makes it easy to see the policy errors that governments are making, and also points to a direction to end business cycles. That view is the theory developed by the economists: Ludwig von Mises, F.A. Hayek and Murray

Rothbard, and which is known as Austrian Business Cycle Theory.

Chapter 4

HOW TO CALCULATE MONEY SUPPLY

The data I use to determine where we are in boom-bust business cycles is largely money supply data. I look at money supply data closely because of my belief that Austrian Business Cycle Theory [34] presents an accurate description of why the business cycle occurs and helps in understanding where in the business cycle an economy is. The primary driver, according to ABCT, of the business cycle is central bank manipulation of the money supply.

The central bank creates money, but that money does not fall into hands of everyone at the same time. Because the money is created via banks, it is the capital good sectors, such as the stock market and real estate, that generally see the newly created money first, and thus it should not come as a surprise that it is the stock market and real estate market that benefit most from the boom phase of the business cycle. And, further, when money growth is slowed, that is during the during the bust phase of the business cycle, the impact is harshest on the same capital goods sectors, e.g., the stock market crashes but not the price of French fries or sodas.

The money supply growth numbers that I calculate are based on the raw data that can be found at the web site of the central bank of the United States, that is, the Federal Reserve web site. Specifically, I use the data found in the H.6 release, Money Stock Measures - H.6. The Fed releases new data every Thursday at 4:30 PM ET.

http://federalreserve.gov/releases/h6/current/default.htm

I use the 13-week averaged quarterly data, provided at H.6, as a rough guide as to when money supply changes have been in effect long enough to have an impact on the economy. I feel compelled to emphasize that the quarterly measure is just a rough rule of thumb that I have developed as a result of monitoring money supply data for decades. If you take a shorter period, you catch too many insignificant changes in money supply. If you look at simple 12 month annualized data, you miss shorter-term growth changes that do have an impact on the stock market and economy.

Specifically, here's what I do: I go to Table 2 of the H.6 release and go to column 10, which is the M2 13-week, non-seasonally adjusted measure of M2. I calculate the percentage change in money growth by taking the earliest week in the data and the most current week and determining the percentage change from the earliest week to the current week. That gives me the quarterly change in money growth. I then raise that rate exponentially by the power of 4 to get an annualized number.

I use non-seasonally adjusted money data as opposed to seasonally adjusted data, since I want to know the exact amount of money out in the system available to bid up prices versus some seasonal adjusted data. You don't dress based on seasonally adjusted weather, you dress on the actual weather conditions. The same holds for money supply. It's the actual money out there bidding up goods and services that is important.

THE FED FLUNKS

APPENDIX

A Note on Money Market Funds and the Calculation of Money Supply

There is one more note with regard to my money supply calculation that is of a technical nature that I want to address here. I am covering this technical note here mostly for students of Austrian school economic theory who may note that I include money market funds as part of the money supply, something that the Austrian economic theorist Murray Rothbard left out in his determination of the money supply.

Here's why I believe it should be included.

The idea that money market funds should not be considered part of the money supply, by Austrian school economists, came about because of a measure of money supply developed by Rothbard, now called the True Money Supply.

In his book, **The Mystery of Banking**[35], Rothbard wrote with regard to money market funds:

> For money market funds rest on short-term credit instruments and they are not legally redeemable at par, much like savings deposits. The difference seems to be that the public holds the savings deposit to be legally redeemable at

par, whereas it realizes that there are inevitable risks attached to the money market fund. Hence, the weight of the argument is against including these goods in the money supply.

But it is curious that in his book, **America's Great Depression**[36], Rothbard included the surrender value of life insurance policies as part of the money supply (my bold):

> Life insurance surrender liabilities are our most controversial suggestion. It cannot be doubted, however, that they can **supposedly** be redeemed at par on demand, and must therefore, according to our principles, be included in the total money supply. The chief differences, for our purposes, between these liabilities and others listed above are that the policyholder is discouraged by all manner of propaganda from cashing in claims, and that the **life insurance company keeps almost none of its assets in cash---roughly between one and two percent.**

It is difficult for me to see how Rothbard could include insurance policies as part of the money supply but not the new development, since he wrote AGD, of money market funds. I would venture to guess that most of the public that holds money market funds sees them as immediately redeemable with no risk, which would meet Rothbard's criteria for money, as he outlined it in AGD.

Indeed, after excluding money market funds from the money supply, Rothbard writes in **The Mystery of Banking**[37]:

The point, however, is that there are good arguments either way on the money market fund, which highlights the grave problem the Fed and the Friedmanites have in zeroing in on one money supply figure for total control.

In other words, he wasn't as hard core against including money market funds as part of the money supply as some would believe.

But a very significant reason as to whether something should be considered part of the money supply is how important an impact the factor hason such things as the capital structure and price fluctuations? Joseph Salerno, who sides with Rothbard in arguing that money market funds should not be counted as part of the money supply, nonetheless, I believe, provides the best argument as to why money market funds should be considered as part of the money supply. He writes in **Money, Sound and Unsound**[38]:

> The existence of MMMFs does have an effect on overall prices in the economy [..]

He adds that this does not mean it is part of the money supply but:

> Rather, the liquidity and checkability features of these assets permit their holders to reduce the amount of money they need to keep on hand to meet anticipated payments and to insure future contingencies.

I would argue that it is simply a case of money being held as money market funds, instead of, say, as demand deposit money, since they pretty much accomplish the same thing. But, further, if one of our goals in watching money supply is to get a sense for what type of price inflation we might expect, and money markets have an impact on prices, then we sure ought to watch what is happening to the size of money market funds, when we are considering money supply.

(Note: Salerno likens money market funds to credit cards, which he says can also impact prices--true to a degree, but I would argue that credit cards are a different animal than money market funds, since a liability is taken on when a credit card is used.)

As for not including small denomination time deposits (CDs), my views are in line with those of Salerno:

> As time deposits, CDs nominally are not cashable on demand, but are payable in dollars only after a contractually fixed period of time ranging from thirty days to a number of years. However, the fact that the issuing institutions stand ready to redeem these liabilities in current dollars at any time prior to maturity does constitute a theoretical argument for their inclusion in TMS [The True Money Supply] at their current redemption value.

Bottom line: It is best to look at the factors that do have a very close impact on prices (either consumer or capital goods prices), and include them as part of the money supply. Money market funds and small-denomination time deposits (CDs) fit this criteria.

NOTES

Live links to all links in the below notes can be found at GallatinHouse.com/FedFlunksNotes

1. Since I have spent most of my career as a financial consultant helping various firms raise money. I have often written under nom de plumes. The last thing I need is blowback against my clients for my attacks on government regulators and banksters. I used a nom de plume when I wrote the Housing piece but disclosed that to Potter and Peach and also at EconomicPolicyJournal.com.

I have assembled a collection of my previous writings that I have written under different names and plan to publish them in book form as soon as my consulting days are over. I am winding down that business and focusing more of my efforts on EconomicPolicyJoural.com and book writing. Watch EconomicPolicyJournal.com for an announcement on when the collection will be published.

2. I have printed my critique of the Peach-McCarthy housing paper as chapter in this booklet.

3. Rothbard, Murray N., *A History of Money and Banking in the United States: The Colonial Era to World War II* (Auburn, Alabama: The Ludwig Von Mises Institute, 2002).

4. The Ludwig von Mises Institute was founded in 1982 as the research and educational center of classical liberalism, libertarian political theory, and the Austrian School of economics. See more at Mises.org

5. Hayek, F.A., *Choice in Currency: A Way to Stop Inflation* (London: The Institute for Economic Affairs, 1976), p. 13.

6. http://www.zerohedge.com/news/robert-wenzels-david-speech-crushes-federal-reserves-goliath-dream

7. See: Hoppe, Hans-Hermann, Economic Science and the Austrian Method, (Auburn, Alabama, The Ludwig von Mises Institute, 2007)

8. Lowenstein, Roger, *When Genius Failed: The Rise and Fall of Long-Term Capital Management*, (New York: Random House Trade Paperbacks, 2001) pp. 95–97

Sorkin, Andrew Ross, *Too Big to Fail* (New York: Penguin Books, 2010), p. 303

10. Murphy, Robert, *The Politically Incorrect Guide to the Great Depression and the New Deal* (Washington, D.C.:Regenery Publishing, Inc,2008)

11.http://www.nobelprize.org/nobel_prizes/economics/la
ureates/2010/press.html

12.ftp://ftp.bls.gov/pub/special.requests/cpi/cpiai.txt

13. Rothbard, Murray N., America's Great Depression (
Auburn, Alabama: The Ludwig von Mises Institue,
2000)

14.http://www.economicpolicyjournal.com/2008/07/sup
er-alert-dramatic-slowdown-in-money.html

15.http://www.economicpolicyjournal.com/2008/07/alert
-collapsing-credit.html

16.http://www.federalreserve.gov/newsevents/speech/ber
nanke20080609a.htm

17.http://epjdailyalert.economicpolicyjournal.com/2014/
04/subscribe-to-epj-daily-alert.html

18.http://www.economicpolicyjournal.com/2008/07/sup
er-alert-dramatic-slowdown-in-money.html

19.http://www.frbsf.org/publications/economics/letter/20
11/el2011-13.html

20.http://www.federalreserve.gov/pubs/feds/200

21.http://www.huffingtonpost.com/2012/04/03/federal-
reserve-watergate-iraqi-weapons_n_1400645.html

22.http://www.federalreserve.gov/releases/h41/Current/

23.http://www.newyorkfed.org/aboutthefed/visiting.html

24.http://fednewyork.org/research/epr/04v10n3/0412mcc
a.pdf

25.http://www.economicpolicyjournal.com/2012/02/che
ckmate-new-york-fed-as-totally.html

26.http://www.nytimes.com/2012/04/25/business/econo
my/survey-shows-us-home-prices-still-weak.html

27.http://www.newyorkfed.org/research/epr/04v10n3/04
12mcca.html

28. http://www.gold-eagle.com/article/1927-1933-chart-
pompous-prognosticators

29. http://www.washingtonpost.com/wp-
dyn/content/article/2010/09/01/AR2010090106148.html
?sid=ST2010090106698

30.http://www.economicpolicyjournal.com/2008/07/sup
er-alert-dramatic-slowdown-in-money.html

31.
http://www.economicpolicyjournal.com/2008/07/alert-
collapsing-credit.html

32.http://www.economicpolicyjournal.com/2008/08/mon
ey-supply-watch-moving-closer-to.html

33.
http://www.economicpolicyjournal.com/2008/09/alert-
money-growth-plunges-to-18.html

34.Rothbard, Murray N., Austrian School Business
Cycle Theory: An Examination of What Causes the
Boom-Bust Business Cycle, (Casper, Wyoming;Gallatin
House, 2014)

35. Rothbard, Murray N. *The Mystery of Banking,*
(Auburn, Alabama The Ludwig von Mises Institute; 2nd
edition 2008) p. 256

36. Murray N. Rothbard, *America's Great Depression,*
pp. 90-91

37. 1. Murray N. Rothbard, *The Mystery of Banking,*
p.256

38 Joseph T. Salerno, *Money, Sound and Unsound,*
((Auburn, AL; Ludwig von Mises Institute; 2011) p. 125

THE FED FLUNKS

Robert Wenzel is the Editor and Publisher of *EconomicPolicyJournal.com*.

He resides in San Francisco.

THE FED FLUNKS

Be sure to visit:

EconomicPoilcyJournal.com for more commentary about the economy.